AF488237

My Favorite Americans:

Drawing Inspiration from Ordinary Lives

Earl Franklin Johnson, Jr.

Lee Ann Johnson Linam

Library of Congress Cataloging-in-Publication Data
Names:
Johnson, Earl Franklin, Jr.; author
Linam, Lee Ann Johnson; author
Title: My Favorite Americans
Subtitle: Drawing Inspiration from Ordinary Lives
Identifiers:
ISBN 979-8-9938696-2-9

Cover photo depicting diverse friends picnicking by the marshlands generated using ChatGPT (OpenAI), 2026.

Dedication

To Euner Lee Griffin Johnson, our wife and mother. Your love, tireless support, and willingness to embrace a wider world opened up the doors to these relationships and helped them flourish.

Frank, Lee Ann, and Euner Johnson, circa 1962.

*Frank Johnson at his desk at Aransas National
Wildlife Refuge*

Foreword – *Lee Ann Johnson Linam*

When my father, Earl Franklin Johnson, Jr., (known to friends and family as "Frank") passed away unexpectedly from a sudden heart attack in 1986, we found the introduction of this book scribbled on a yellow legal pad in a drawer of his work desk. He provided us with a list of names but had not completed his thoughts about these unique individuals. Some we knew well. Others we did not, so we did our best to track down these individuals or their families and friends. In the process we were not only inspired by their character, but we were drawn closer to my father's character. The introduction is in my father's words, while the remaining chapters are me, his daughter, trying to tell the stories of the relationships he experienced.

We don't know for sure if my father would have added other "characters" to this list. Certainly, our family was blessed with numerous friends from many walks of life. In the end, I decided to simply pursue the initial list of people that we found scribbled on that yellow pad. Though my father titled this collection "My Favorite Americans," the people are not all American citizens—another reflection of his belief in what makes America great.

Table of Contents

My Favorite Americans:

An Introduction

-Earl Franklin Johnson, Jr.

I have been bird-watching with Lady Bird Johnson and "chowed down" many times with one of the richest men in Texas, Toddie Lee Wynne, Jr. I have ridden in the Governor of Texas's helicopter and flown over barrier islands with Perry Bass, among the Who's Who of wealthy Americans, after spending time at his very private San Jose Island retreat. I have seen President John Kennedy and visited the ranch of President Lyndon Johnson. State Senators and Representatives have spoken from the same podium as I.

Each of these famous Americans can be read about in many books and periodicals. This little book is not about such people. Thinking back on the back roads I have traveled, I do not remember and have not been impressed as much by the famous and rich as by many, many other faces I have seen along these roads.

These are common folks with little money but big in heart, rich in family, ready to share their last dime, neighborly people and the backbone of America. These faces flash across your memory and bring a smile to your face or a tear to your eye. Many have been laughed at by others, called no good by some, and shunned by still others. I wonder is it because they are "different" or perhaps because they live in that less-than-comfortable home, drive a 1956 pickup, or drink a six pack of Miller Lite each day?

My family and I, while having one of our many laughter-filled family "silly sessions," said, "Wouldn't it be fun to have a party and invite our interesting and different guest list?" Thus, we began to list all the real people who have crossed our paths. As the list developed, we were further inspired to write a mini-biography of their faces along the road.

No bigotry, injustice, slander, or other malice is intended against anyone. On the contrary, much love, appreciation, and thanks go to the selected few for making our life a little bit richer and a lot more fun. After all, what's life for, if not to get to know those that really make America great?

"Some people strengthen the society just by being the kind of people they are."
-James W. Gardner.

"The greatness of a man can nearly always be measured by his willingness to be kind."
-G. Young

"Great Spirit, help me never to judge another until I have walked in his moccasins."
-Sioux Indian Prayer

"We must not drift away from the humble works, because these are the works nobody will do. It is never too small. We are so small we look at things in a small way. But God, being Almighty, sees everything great...Very humble work, that is where you and I must be. For there are many people who can do big things. But there are very few people who will do the small things."
-Mother Teresa of Calcutta

Family "silly session" outside our home on Aransas National Wildlife Refuge.

Chapter 1 – Dedication

Blind and Gator – McClellanville, South Carolina

-Based on an interview with Ned Jaycocks -
September 2016

My family's path intersected with the lives of Blind and Gator when my father served as refuge manager at Cape Romain National Wildlife Refuge from 1963-67. The bayous, marsh islands, and Spanish moss-clad live oak woods of the central South Carolina coast produced many colorful residents, and, according to local resident Ned Jaycock, these working men left impressions on many residents beyond my father in the small fishing town of McClellanville.

Gator's given name was James E. Turner, Jr., but he had several nicknames, including "Doogie, "Cap'n Ned," and "Gator"—the one he preferred. He was the son of J.E. Turner of the small community of Wren's Chapel. Gator had a very rudimentary upbringing and essentially no formal education. Eventually, he fell into the profession of painter, a job often associated with drunkenness, but Gator was known for his dependability, and when refuge manager Edgar Jaycock hired him as a laborer at Cape Romain, Gator was forever thankful for a good job. His love for and loyalty to the wildlife refuge was renowned. No one knows the source of the nickname he embraced. It may have originated from his multi-faceted love for wetland creatures. When my Dad arrived at Cape Romain, Gator informed him, "We just take a turtle every once in a whiles, when we need one..." We're not sure whether my father's redirect of that prohibited activity was successful. However, the alligators, turtles, and legends of Gator still persist in rural Charlestown County.

Gator's grave marker in his home community of Wren's Chapel reflects his love for his work at Cape Romain Refuge

Blind, born Isaac Geathers, was another laborer on Cape Romain Refuge. Ned Jaycocks, whose father preceded my father as manager of Cape Romain Refuge, reported that Blind predated their family's arrival in 1955—making him seem a timeless fixture in the boats and shops of the refuge. Unlike Gator, who never married or had children, Blind (whose nickname source was also unknown, as he was sighted) wed to his beloved Clara and produced 16 children and over 100 grandchildren. The Geathers developed a close relationship with the Jaycock family. Though I never learned much about my father's relationship with Blind, Ned Jaycock noted that Blind was particularly known for his "pearls of wisdom," an attribute that put him on my father's list, I am sure.

Blind sitting on his porch in coastal South Carolina.

Chapter 2 – Optimism

Daris Ann Nowell – Weir, Mississippi

My grandmother, Maw-maw, lived next door to Daris in Weir, Mississippi. There are many traditions vivid in my memory from our semi-annual visits back to my father's tiny hometown—hiking down the railroad track to the swimming hole on the creek, poking through the woods to find the bubbling white sand of a local spring, spending our allowance at the candy counter of the "downtown" drug store, and going next door to visit Daris and Helen in their classic southern home where they lived with their elderly mother. Helen was always quietly friendly, but Daris always had plenty to say!

As a child, I never knew Daris's age. She was nearly my parents' age, but, in her irrepressible enthusiasm, she seemed much younger. Maybe Daris was just young at heart. Even into her 60s, she dressed in short shorts and halter tops, consistently applied bright makeup, and kept her bottle-enhanced, jet-black hair styled in the latest fashion. She proudly told us a story of someone "mistaking" her for Cheryl Prewitt, the 1980 Miss America from just down the road in Ackerman. Prewitt was about 20 years her junior, but that didn't stop Daris from believing and cherishing a stranger's light-hearted, kind remark. Instead, she told us that Miss America had a much more pointed chin than she did. Daris was gracious about the "flaw."

Daris' ability to tell stories was legendary. She would share news of everyone in town, her fluffy white dog and collection of neighborhood cats, her visits to her nieces in Florida (people we felt like we should know, even if we didn't), and all kinds of popular culture, as if tiny Weir kept up with LA and NYC.

While sitting in the un-air-conditioned, high-ceilinged visiting room of their home, listening to Daris seamlessly transition from one story to the next, my sleepy mind would become overwhelmed with the chatter, and my attention would drift to bric-a-brac from a bygone era scattered on doilies leaving intricate dust rings on antique furniture. I struggled to keep my eyes open and nod some affirmation. When my grandmother tired of Daris's endless musings, she wasn't always so charitable. As Daris would go on and on during a visit to her home, Maw-maw would often abruptly say, "Daris, I'm tired. It's time for you to go home now."

And yet, Daris always kept an eye out for Maw-maw. Perhaps motivated at least partially by curiosity, Daris would always fetch my grandmother's mail and bring it to her house. Ever vigilant to emerging "news," she conveniently could see my Maw-maw's bedroom windows from her own and would check on Maw-maw if her light came on at night. One night, my aunt's family arrived late at night, and Maw-maw got her gun, fearing intruders (Maw-maw was a character in her own right!). Thankfully, vigilant Daris called my grandmother to share the news that Betty and Bob had arrived.

Daris' world was not expansive. She never had children, never spoke of a long-ended marriage, never lived outside a two-county area in Central Mississippi, and never won the Miss America or any other pageant, but she left her mark on her world. After her passing, I asked a local resident in a Weir café whether he knew Daris. He said everyone knew Daris and Helen. He told of her walking all around town, picking up litter, and talking to anyone she met. He recalled how she and Helen habitually took in stray dogs and cats. Overhearing us speak, the owners of the local Sunflower Food Store in Weir simply said, "Everyone loved Daris."

Daris and my brothers exploring the seep spring that once provided water to many households in Weir, Mississippi.

Chapter 3 - Wisdom

Sam Huff, Sr. - Austwell, Texas

-Based on an interview with Sam Huff, Jr. –
May 15, 2016

Sam Huff, Sr., lived on Vandenberge Street in the tiny town of Austwell, Texas, when our family knew him. He would sit on the porch of his clapboard house, watching the (very light) traffic go by, and that's where my Dad would find him each day as he made the 7-mile drive from Aransas National Wildlife Refuge to Austwell's tiny post office. Daddy would stop by and talk about the things of the world, at least their world, with Sam—sharing stories from the town and the refuge and reckoning that the two of them had the answers to everything.

Sam Huff's grandparents arrived on the Texas Gulf coast from the Gulfport-Biloxi, Mississippi, area soon after the Emancipation Proclamation, settling on Blackjack Peninsula. For decades, the family resided on the peninsula, then a private ranch, now Aransas Refuge, working as cowhands and later finding a little supplementary income bootlegging during the Prohibition era. Game and fish were plentiful, especially Canada geese, doves, and quail. The family would catch fish on ribbons called "drop-lines" and hunt raccoons for their hides. When the family arrived, Karankawa Indians were still in the area, and the family traded with them.

Sam's father and mother, Wesley and Laura, had seven boys and two girls, including Sam who was born in 1903. By the 1920s, Sam found employment with the railroad in Austwell as a brakeman. His travels on the railroad shipping cotton, corn, and sorghum up and down the Texas coast led him to Brazoria, where he met his future wife, Cordelia. The couple bought a lot in Austwell in 1933 from the Bluhm family and built their first home.

The city was a bustling agricultural community then, with a cotton gin, grain elevator, mercantile, four or five cafes, a dry-cleaner, and "The World's Largest Shell Pile"—oyster shell excavated from the bay that was used to build roads in the area. (Sam, Jr. reported that the kids in his day used the shell dug-out area in Hynes Bay as their swimming hole.) Sam ran a café called "Four-Wheel Drive-In" in Austwell and worked at roofing and fencing and as a caretaker on the Schindler Farm, not far outside town.

Sam and Cordelia raised four girls and three boys. Sam, Jr. recalls a diverse group of friends, but in the 1940s and 1950s, the town had two schools for students up to junior high school, segregated by race. White students could continue high school in nearby Tivoli, while black students had to travel over 30 miles to Refugio for high school. Still, Austwell circumvented segregation during the summer when unofficial summer school was provided by Miss Winnie, a matriarch of the community. Miss Winnie, truly an Austwell fixture, was even interviewed by the producers of the mini-series "Roots." According to Sam, Jr., Miss Winnie taught, guided, and spanked the community's young people, both white and black!

In Sam Huff, Sr., I think my father found a richness of life and a collection of life experiences that often go unappreciated. He valued the common humanity and simple wisdom that their frequent conversations revealed. Sam passed away suddenly on June 3, 1986. My father was away on business then and mourned that he could not attend his funeral, but even more, he mourned that his friend would no longer be there for their daily chats. Instead, until his own untimely death later that year, Daddy would throw up his hand and say, "Hi, Sam!" as he passed the simple black cemetery on the way from Austwell back to Aransas National Wildlife

Refuge, where my Dad perhaps walked the very paths Sam walked as a young man.

The Huff legacy continues in Austwell and nearby communities today. Sam, Jr., a welder and Vietnam veteran, lived on the same street as his father. Sam Sr. would have been proud to know that several of his grandchildren went on to finish college and work as nurses and coaches. And sometimes my family still says "Hi, Sam!" as we pass the site of his old house.

Sunrise over Hines Bay in Austwell, swimming spot for generations of Huffs.

Chapter 4 – Nonconformity

Spirit – Everywhere and Nowhere

Spirit wandered into our lives sometime in the late 1970s. Although non-motorists sometimes reached Aransas National Wildlife Refuge, with the refuge entrance 12 miles from the nearest highway and over 30 miles from the closest mid-sized town, it wasn't common. And yet, one day, Spirit just appeared.

Spirit called himself an "adventurer, wanderer, philosopher, and orphan." We never knew his real name, but his aspect fitted his self-ascribed moniker. Wearing long hair, beads, and baggy cotton clothes and carrying nothing but a small backpack, he reminded me of the downtown Atlanta hippies our family cruised by in the late 1960s just to gawk at the novelty. Here was the same type of character in rural Texas a decade later. Always with a soft spot for the nonconformist, my Dad broke a few rules and let Spirit escape the Aransas humidity and mosquitoes in a small sleeping quarter for work crews. (We all also secretly hoped that Spirit would avail himself of the shower facility there...).

From that point, Spirit inserted himself into our family. He instructed us in his balance philosophy—the Male and the Female, the Big and the Little, the Hot and the Cold, and the Fire and the Water. With his stringy long hair, unkept beard, and androgynous clothing, he portrayed the Male and the Female (though, in my teenage discomfort, I did manage to dodge his requests for me to add femininity by French-braiding his hair). The Big and the Little were displayed in a unique, almost indecipherable penmanship he had developed using curlicued upper-case and lower-case letters mixed together randomly. To my mother's chagrin, his experimentations with the Hot and the Cold one day produced an inedible fruit dessert—as Spirit thought that the unbaked pie crust he found in our refrigerator would be best served cold during the hot summer.

The most dramatic story of the Fire and the Water reached us later after Spirit left us, as we heard from a law enforcement friend how Spirit had been brought up before a South Texas judge (presumably on suspicion of being suspicious). Spirit perceived that the unfriendly judge had too much fire and proceeded to "baptize" him by throwing water at him. Thankfully, our friend had met Spirit and convinced the judge that he was harmless despite his nonconformist lifestyle and surprising behavior.

Spirit would stay at Aransas for a week or two and then wander to other locations before reappearing months or years later. My father welcomed him back every time, even as others looked askance. Each time, Spirit would share new reflections of his "insights" that remain in our family's vocabulary to this day. We didn't hear from Spirit for an extended period and began to worry about him, but those worries were pushed aside in a poignant moment. We lost my father suddenly to a heart attack in 1986. And then Spirit re-emerged, sending word of his condolences to my family, letting us know that our father's open-hearted kindness lived on in a long-haired adventurer, wanderer, philosopher, and orphan.

Chat GPT's conception of Spirit's visit to us at the refuge. He wasn't really quite that tidy. (OpenAI, 2026.)

Chapter 5 – Faithfulness

Rev. Mack Williams – Tivoli, Texas

*-Based on interviews with Reverend Mack
and his great-nephew Irwin Williams*

Reverend Mack was one of our first acquaintances when we moved to Texas. Mack worked for my father at Aransas Refuge, but he also quickly became a life-long family friend.

Mack was born on the O'Connor San Antonio River Ranch in Refugio County, Texas, on November 16, 1914, to Butler and Emma Williams. Mack's paternal grandfather, Thornton Williams, was brought to the central coastal prairies of Texas as an enslaved person by the William O'Connor family. With a family that dated back to frontier Texas, Mack heard stories about how Karankawa chased his grandfather into the bay, but, interestingly, his grandfather married a Cherokee woman, Fanny, who had been captured in a raid. Fanny knew Cherokee traditional medicine and passed it down to her grandchildren. Mack's maternal grandparents were Isaiah and Frances Weathers. Isaiah came to Texas from Virginia, was a preacher, and started many churches. Frances Youngblood's family was from Louisiana. Mack did not know all the history of his maternal grandparents. However, he shared the story of how his mother figured out her age by recollecting how she aided Union soldiers when they came through their area in 1862.

Mack's father cowboyed and managed horses and veterinary work for the O'Conner Ranch. "Buzzard," as he was called, ended up on the Peach Mott Unit working for Martin O'Conner, with whom he was raised. In his later years, after horseback injuries, he became a cook. Butler and Emma had ten children and lived in a section of the ranch that came to be known as Butler Mott. Their neighbors were ranch hands, mostly of Mexican heritage, so Mack grew up speaking more Spanish than English. The Williams boys were a rowdy bunch—known for gambling and carousing in the small nearby community of Tivoli. The not-yet "reverend" Mack used to take food to his brothers when they would end up in the Tivoli jail.

Mack Williams, on right, with two other O'Connor Ranch cowboys in the 1940s. Photo # 095-0310-General Photograph Collection - UTSA Digital Collections. Courtesy of Rev. Mack and Alice Mae Williams.

Mack met his future wife, Alice Mae Barefield, born on the neighboring McFaddin Ranch, when she was four. Always joking, he described her as being quiet and as wide as she was tall, but one day, he picked her up and told his mother, "That's who I am going to marry." The two went to school together in Tivoli. Mack and his siblings would stay with an uncle in Tivoli during the five month-long school year but would leave when the cotton season started or if they were needed for ranch work.

True to his word, Mack married Alice Mae when she was 14. Like his father, he worked as a cowboy on the O'Connor ranch, while Alice Mae worked as a cook on the ranch. Mack's nickname was El Coyote Prieto (The Dark Coyote). He said he got the nickname because he was famous for getting drunk and coming home and howling outside the door. Mack tells with a wink the story of one night when he arrived home howling very late to a very angry Alice Mae. According to Mack's story, a marital scuffle ensued. The outcome of the "scufflin' and wrestlin'" was Alice Mae "beggin' and beggin.'" She was begging him to "come out from under that bed, you coward!" Aside from scuffles with Alice Mae, cowboy work was rough, and Mack suffered several broken ribs. Though several of his brothers and brothers-in-law served in World War II, Mack's employers wanted to retain his services, so, despite his protests, they prepared an affidavit noting that he was needed for agricultural work.

In 1945 at a preaching meeting at the age of 31, Mack decided the Dark Coyote needed to stop howling and follow Jesus—a new relationship that affected the pattern of the rest of his life. He began preaching at the church on the ranch and took a job

Reverend Mack conducting a baptism in the San Antonio River near Tivoli in the early 1960s. Photo # 096-1167- General Photograph Collection - UTSA Digital Collections. Courtesy:Rev Mack and Alice Mae Williams.

at the Tivoli Mercantile, though the ranch would still call for his help when moving cattle. Preacher Mack wanted to improve his English grammar, so he began attending Conroe Normal & Industrial College Advanced Education for African Americans, a school founded in 1903 to provide higher education to black students during segregation. Later, he switched and began attending Corpus Christi State University, carpooling from Tivoli with other local students. In 1951, Mack started pastoring at Mt. Galilee Baptist Church in Tivoli and at St. Paul Baptist in Victoria in 1961. He also preached at Bethlehem Baptist in Austwell and at ranch churches on the Wells Ranch and Vidaurri Ranch.

Reverend Mack was a fixture in the Austwell-Tivoli Community. After leaving work at the mercantile, he served as head custodian at two schools in Tivoli, establishing friendships with a whole generation of schoolchildren. From there, he went to work at Aransas National Wildlife Refuge. Mack was an integral part of the refuge family. He took on any maintenance or cleaning task assigned. He was famous for his sparkling clean restrooms), but he was also frequently requested to speak to school groups. My father said that when schools called to schedule their field trips, if Reverend Mack wasn't available to lead the tour, they would reschedule for when he was! In Mack's retirement, he fondly recalled the great work environment and the enjoyment staff would have after hours, eating wild hogs, pitching horseshoes, and telling tales. Mack actually retired *twice* from the refuge after 24 total years of service. My Dad said that if he could have found funding to keep Mack employed simply as a storyteller, he would have done it; Mack added that much charisma and flavor to the refuge for its visitors and staff.

Rev. Mack Williams driving tractor at Aransas National Wildlife Refuge. Photo # 096-1119-General Photograph Collection - UTSA Digital Collections. Courtesy: Rev. Mack and Alice Mae Williams.

Indeed, everyone who knew Reverend Mack knew he was full of stories. Able to immerse the listener in the colorful story of life on Texas ranches, Mack was widely interviewed. He was one of the cowhands featured in Louise O'Connor's local history work, *Cryin' for Daylight: A Ranching*

Culture in the Texas Coastal Bend, and his voice recordings are found in the Institute of Texan Cultures. He told how the cowboys would undress to swim across the river and then redress. He told the story of Uncle Jimmy, who worked on the ranch but always wore a necktie and women's high heels. And then there was the story of the time he shot nine wild geese with one shot on the ranch and was mad because he wanted to go to town but had to delay and pick all those geese!

Mack was also famous for recounting colorful stories at Aransas. He once reported to refuge biologist Tom Stehn that a *monkey* had been sighted from the top of the refuge observation tower. Tom hurried down to check out the sighting. He didn't find a monkey, but, for some inexplicable, perhaps salacious, reason he did spot two pairs of women's underwear in the tree branches. The next day Mack showed up at the refuge headquarters with a tame coatimundi he befriended—a pet that someone had released on the refuge. Perhaps the coatimundi explained the monkey sighting, but the women's panties remain a mystery to this day. One day Mack told us about the evening he *felt* the presence of a mountain lion and that his hair and his hat lifted up off his head, even before he saw it!

Mack and Alice Mae had two children—Roy, who was killed in a truck accident in the 1960s, and Mack, Jr., who died from cancer—and four grandchildren. But they raised many others, including Irwin and his siblings, who came to live with Mack and Alice Mae in 1960 after their mother died. Family members knew him affectionately as "Uncle Teat," a name not shared in public. He loved barbecuing, a skill he passed on to his nephew Irwin. Some of his most memorable life events were visiting Washington D.C. and the East and West Coasts.

Though Alice Mae was quiet, Reverend Mack was a people person. He was active in the local Lions Club and was a fixture as the emcee of the annual Independence Day parade. He was also the presiding judge for unofficial horse races afterward (where he perhaps overlooked the fact that a homely gray gelding ridden by an enthusiastic preteen girl—myself—always broke the starting line). When our family arrived in Texas in 1973, Mack was our first Spanish teacher. Our lack of proficiency was no reflection of his entertaining instructional style. He was notoriously generous. When my father died unexpectedly, Reverend Mack drew us away from the deep sorrow of the funeral home and took the whole extended family out to a seafood restaurant. My future Great Aunt Effie Pridgen protested when he refused to split the bill. Still, the only contribution Mack would accept was a donation to his church. As the community later gathered for a memorial service to honor my father, we knew without hesitation that we wanted to ask Reverend Mack to share wisdom and remembrances. From one life well-lived to another.

Reverend Mack on his second retirement from Aransas National Wildlife Refuge.

Chapter 6 – Creativity

Roberto Andrea Rossi – Como, Italy

Roberto came into our family's life in 1985 through the American Foreign Service high school student exchange program. AFS, a phenomenal program for building bridges and sharing cultural appreciation, usually places students in an environment that fits their interests in a somewhat familiar setting. Indeed, in 1984, their decision to place a student from a Netherlands farming community with our family on a national wildlife refuge was a great fit. Wim Twisk reveled in hog hunting on the refuge, boating and fishing, visiting local ranches, high school sports, and biking the vast expanses of Aransas National Wildlife Refuge. Wim tried to teach us to speak Dutch, and we tried to get him to eat American cheese. Despite those mutual failures, our time together created a close bond and friendship between our families that lasts to this day.

But not all AFS students are the same, and when Roberto, a writer, musician, and engineering enthusiast, got off the plane a year later from Como, a populous fashion and arts center in northern Italy, and found himself landed in Tivoli, population 600, there were some adjustments to be made. In Roberto's words, the students at Austwell-Tivoli High School found him "interesting." At the same time, Roberto thought he must have encountered the original Tuna, Texas.

Roberto's experiences in our small community gave him plenty of stories to take home to Como. Rumors flew when he embraced the not-unusual European practice of converting underwear into swim trunks in the local bay. One time he heard relationship innuendos hurtful to a female friend at the high school, so he planted a "secret" note to absolve his friend and supplant the story with even juicier but less harmful gossip about himself. When fund-raising chocolates started disappearing from his school locker, he started supplementing them with laxatives so the thief might have second thoughts. Despite his creative comebacks, the discomfort of the misfit assignment began to wear on him, and he came to our home for respite as a new AFS assignment was sought.

Instead of trying to reform Roberto, my father embraced his unique attributes. Despite the rural setting, Roberto found many ways to be creative in our home. He converted an antique crank telephone into a working phone. Tired of the sticky keys on our old upright piano, my mother came home one day to find the 88 hammers and dampers scattered across the living room carpet. (Roberto successfully put the piano back together, but it still sticks today.) Roberto found his greatest enjoyment in using my Dad's early electric typewriter to create stories. Though eventually Roberto transferred to an AFS family in urban Houston, his short time at our home gave us many laughs and remembrances.

Roberto's life continues to embrace creativity—He has worked as an entertainer at a resort in Greece, served as a vocal and drama coach, free-lanced in electronic design, practiced hypnotherapy, set up opportunities for performers through event planning, and even taught computer science to high school students. Despite the mixed AFS experiences, he revisits Texas as often as possible. We like to think he has a little bit of Aransas and my Dad still in him. After a recent WhatsApp conversation, Roberto sent me a picture of a gift my father gave him—some cowboy boots and a western shirt still hanging in his current closet in Malta.

Roberto (in white traditional Italian clothing) creating laughter at an AFS event

Roberto embracing his Texas experience. To this day, he still has those boots given to him by my father.

Chapter 7 – Strength

Madalena Yañez Gomez – Tivoli, Texas

Madalena was born in 1937 in Bonnie View, a tiny farming community carved from a ranch in rural Refugio County, Texas. She was one of eight kids from a blended family with several marriages resulting from widowhood and divorce. Her father was a farmer, raising corn, sorghum, cotton, pigs, and chickens. She attended Bonnie View Elementary School and Woodsboro High School. However, soon after starting high school, her mother died, and Madalena went to live with her grandmother in Richmond, Texas.

At 18, Madalena met and married Luciano Gomez and returned to Refugio County, settling on a farm located between the small towns of Tivoli and Austwell. She and Luciano raised nine children, including six boys and three girls, living in a small, simple frame lease house on the farm where Luciano worked as a farm hand, with a heavy dose of hunting, fishing, and relaxation on the side.

Madalena's work ethic was legendary. At 16, she left school in Richmond to begin cleaning houses and caring for children for $12 weekly. She worked as a janitor and bus driver at Austwell-Tivoli ISD. She loved the outdoors, so my father sought her out when Aransas National Wildlife Refuge needed a firm, hard-working, multi-skilled supervisor for the new Young Adult Conservation Corps, also known as YACC. The program's goal was to accomplish construction and maintenance on the wildlife refuge. It also sought to invest in the lives of young people who had yet to establish a steady work pattern. Madalena assured my father she knew "what it takes to be a boss," and she was right. She led young people in building boardwalks on the Dagger Point and Big Tree trails, erecting steel beams for maintenance buildings, pouring concrete and drilling foundations for the new visitors' center, and in the daily hard labor needed to maintain roads, buildings, and trails in a humid, mosquito-infested environment. Madalena led by example and set her standards high. When she felt her own son fell short, she even fired him! Even while working, she volunteered in the community—being recognized with my father and other community volunteers for their leadership in helping Austwell win a South Texas community improvement award in 1985.

After the YACC program ended, my father continued to call Madalena when the refuge had short-term contract jobs, but eventually she went on to shatter more stereotypes. She became the first female member of the County Commissioner maintenance crew, walking into a skeptical maintenance shop on the first day and retiring with every good ol' boy's admiration and respect. In retirement, Madalena's hands were never still, even as widowhood left her on her own—providing support for her children when they needed it, occasionally taking in some of her 10 grandchildren to raise, always sewing, crocheting, embroidering...she was even making gifts for friends the week that cancer finally overcame her.

If our family were to choose one word to describe Madalena, it would be strength. Not just physical strength (though many respected that attribute in her!) but also strength of character. Born into humble means and losing a mother early, she went to work. Entering young into a marriage that was full of physical, financial, and emotional challenges, she never gave up. Confronted with skepticism in taking on jobs that were "men's work" to support her family, she proved her skeptics wrong. Facing the loss of husband and two children, she never lost faith but continued to give. And the hard work never overcame her ability to find joy— my father could always count on her to join him in celebrating life with a turn on the dance "floor" at the Austwell Fourth of July street dance. Thanks, Madalena, for teaching my family strength with joy.

Madalena (#3) with the Young Adult Conservation Corps crew she led on Aransas NWR

Chapter 8 – Hospitality

Frank Johnson

And what of the book's original author, my beloved father, who created this list of characters and collection of friends?

Earl Franklin Johnson, Jr., was born in McCool, Mississippi, to rural mail carrier E.F. Johnson, Sr., and Myrtle Reed Johnson. Raised in the small communities of McCool and Weir, Frank went on to earn a degree in forestry at Mississippi State University. After gaining experience with the Mississippi Forest Service and serving two years in the U.S. Army, Frank began his career with the U.S. Fish and Wildlife Service in 1958 at White River National Wildlife Refuge (NWR) in Arkansas. While on a trip home from White River he met Euner Lee Griffin of small-town Decatur, Mississippi, who happened to be teaching high school English in Weir. A long-distance courtship began, starting with an invitation to pop popcorn at my grandmother's house and culminating with marriage in 1960.

Frank's career in the Fish and Wildlife Service took to him from White River to Noxubee (now Sam Hamilton) NWR in Mississippi (where I was born), Wapanocca NWR in Arkansas, Washington D.C., Cape Romain NWR in South Carolina (where my brother Stephen was born), the regional office in Atlanta, Georgia (where my brother Greg was born), and, finally, Aransas NWR in Texas, famous as the wintering grounds for the endangered whooping crane. Everywhere he went, my father's welcoming spirit opened his heart and home to the beautiful diversity of friends described in this essay.

My father could have easily pursued multiple career promotions in regional and national offices; however, his first love was serving on refuges in small communities. Pursuing relationships and finding peace of existence were more important to him than career advancement. Satisfied with simple rural settings, he was notorious for failing to use all (or even most) of his federal employee vacation time. Simultaneously, he was never too busy at work to make time for everyone. Reverend Mack fondly recalled that he and my father shared a cup of coffee each morning. Refuge biologist Tom Stehn shared that he could see into my father's office from his own and was somewhat taken aback that he could often see Frank relaxing with his feet up on his desk, leaning back, and seemingly doing "absolutely nothing." Tom noted that, "I quickly learned how that behavior was not only acceptable; it was smart. Not a minute would go by before Frank's phone would ring or someone would walk into his office, and he would deal with whatever issue had come up. There was no time to work on projects, so Frank simply relaxed until the next interruption." Tom realized that my father took on the burden of administration so that others could enjoy focusing on their jobs.

Another friend and employee, Louise Frasier observed in a eulogy for my father that he allowed his employees room enough to be self-starters, but that he was always there to listen. She noted, "He may have been laid back, but somehow he was always a step ahead of you at the finish." Even cut short, his professional finish accomplished a milestone. My dad shared with Tom Stehn that he hoped the population of whooping cranes, which was 47 when we moved to Aransas in 1973, would reach 100 in the winter of 1986-87. Poignantly, on the day my father died, unknown to him, Tom and the U.S. Fish and Wildlife Service pilot had just counted over 100 whoopers in their aerial survey.

Famous for his tousled red hair and ready laughter, including a willingness to laugh at himself, my father was never afraid to meet a new person and never slow to serve in community. George Archibald, founder of the International Crane

Foundation, frequently recalls with great humor the time that my father was asked to say a few words about Aransas NWR at a board meeting for ICF, an organization that carries out bird conservation all over the world. My father cracked up the well-heeled donors attending the dinner in Baraboo, Wisconsin, by thanking them all for coming "just to see me." But in truth, most of Frank Johnson's service was much more local with much less fanfare. In his 13 too-short years at Aransas, my father served as the PTA president for the tiny Class B school district, as the president of the local community improvement organization for Austwell (population 284), as the founder of the local AFS Exchange Program chapter, as treasurer and pianist (even after losing part of a thumb) for the local Methodist congregation of 10-15, as an organizer and Little League coach for teams that played in homemade uniforms, and as a good friend to many.

Louise Frasier described my father as a simple man—requiring little or nothing for himself. In her words, "he felt he wasn't placed on this earth to impress people, but to serve. This included young or old, black, brown, or white." Indeed, our home was open to friends of all ages and all types from all around the world. My two brothers and I knew that no subject was taboo and no question was unwelcome. Though he passed away too soon at age

54, my humble father left behind a trail of public service and scores of friends both near and far from all cultures and walks of life who testified to his welcoming spirit. And he left us with the idea of this book. Many years have passed since Daddy's untimely death, but the largeness of his spirit continues to inspire all of us who shared life with him. It is hard to match the ease with which he built relationships and found beauty in people of all types, but he inspired us to try.

His wife of 26 years, Euner Lee Griffin Johnson, jotted down some of the precepts that guided his life and relationships. Perhaps that's a starting point for all of us.

Precepts of Frank

- Don't go to bed with anger—with family or with anyone (She told the story of how one night he drove 7 miles into town to settle things with the irascible treasurer of the church, even though it was unpleasant.)
- Don't stay away from church or any place of sacred importance because of any person.
- No meeting that is worth your time should be boring. Joy and goodwill should be apparent.
- Never shirk responsibilities in any activity or project.

- Be pleased to share any commendable action of someone not expected. Recognize the goodness in all people.
- Guide youth to leadership when young, and they will embrace it as adults.
- Most of all....laugh!

Though my father's career encompassed exciting work, such as sea turtle conservation in South Carolina, he always valued the human side of wildlife work.

My Dad, Frank Johnson, with a childhood friend in
Mississippi, circa 1939.

More friends from around the world

A teacher visiting Aransas from China

A Mexican biologist visiting Aransas

Teaching Wim, the Dutch exchange student who lived with us on the refuge, to make homemade ice cream.

Frank Johnson (with typical humorous expression) and Louise Frasier accept the plaque recognizing Austwell as the most improved community in Texas in 1977. They won the award again in 1985.

My Dad at Aransas National Wildlife Refuge, his final assignment, with visitors enjoying the observation tower.